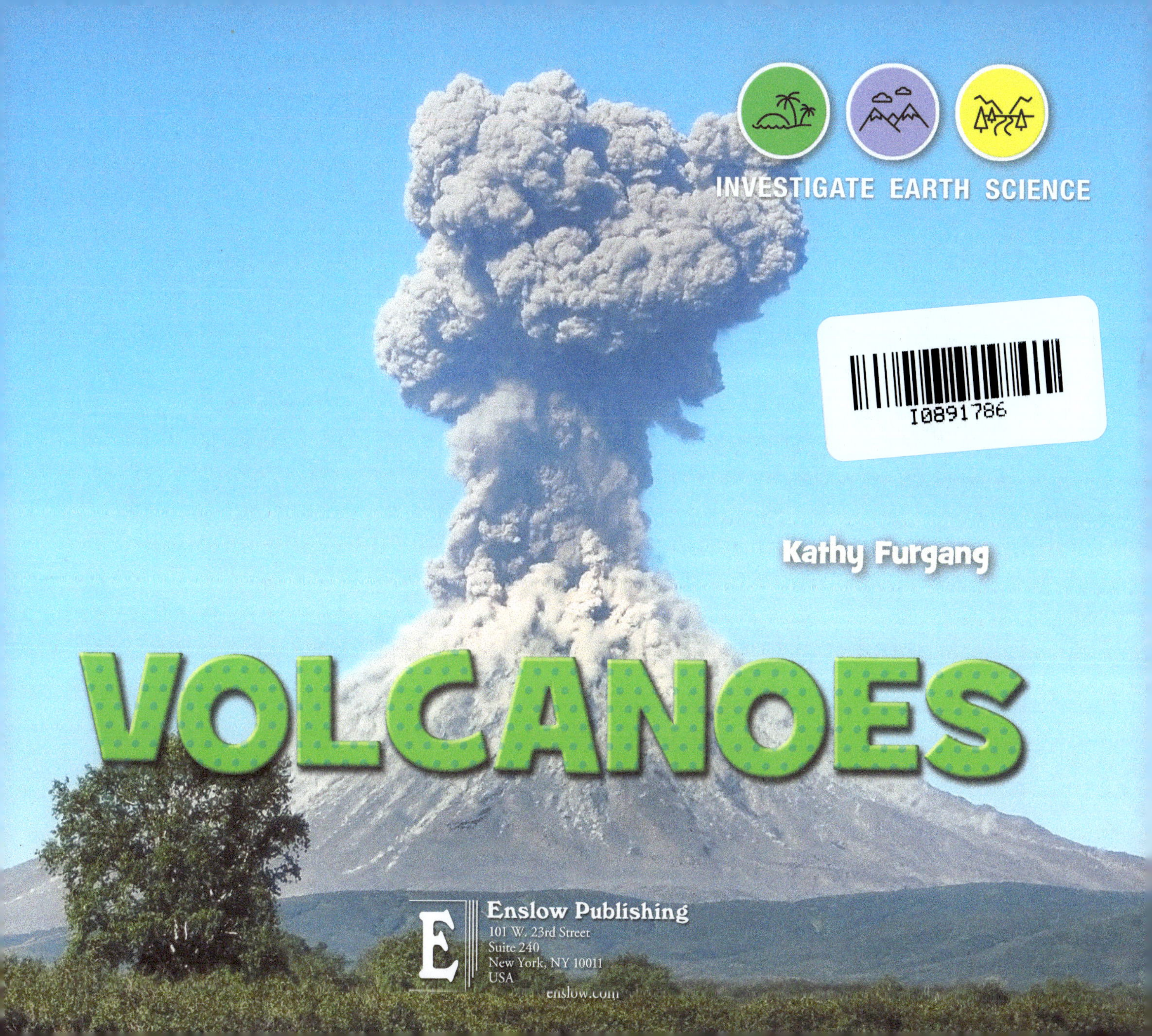

INVESTIGATE EARTH SCIENCE

Kathy Furgang

VOLCANOES

Enslow Publishing
101 W. 23rd Street
Suite 240
New York, NY 10011
USA
enslow.com

Words to Know

crust The outer layer of the earth's surface.

debris Pieces that are left behind when something is destroyed.

ecosystem A community of living things.

eruption An explosion.

fault A break in the earth's crust where large blocks of land shift past each other.

hot spot An area deep under the crust where heat and magma rise to the surface.

lava Magma that has reached through the earth's crust.

magma Hot melted rock underneath the earth's crust.

plate A part of the earth's surface that pieces together with others to form the entire crust.

volcano An opening in the earth's crust where magma reaches the surface as lava.

Contents

Volcanoes in the Making

What makes a **volcano** different from a mountain? The action, of course! Volcanoes look like ordinary mountains. But once in a while, they erupt. When that happens, they show just how active—and dangerous—volcanoes can be. **Lava**, gases, and ash suddenly burst through the earth's **crust**. One volcanic **eruption** can change a landscape within seconds!

Volcanoes are openings in the earth's crust that allow **magma** to reach the surface. Magma is melted liquid rock that is found in the earth's interior. Magma that reaches the earth's surface is called lava. Out of the 1,500 volcanoes on the earth, about 50 erupt each year.

Lava bursts through the earth's crust when a volcano erupts.

Types of Volcanoes

How are all volcanoes alike? They all have a passage down the center, called a vent. The vent is a long opening that allows magma to push all the way up through the crust. How are volcanoes different? There are two main types of volcanoes. Each is known for a different type of eruption.

Red Hot!

Lava is super hot. It reaches up to temperatures three times hotter than a pizza oven! That's up to 2,200° Fahrenheit, or 1,200° Celsius.

Stratovolcano

Shield volcano

Notice the differences between the composite (stratovolcano) and the shield volcano.

A shield volcano is low and wide. Lava bubbles up the vent. Then it slowly flows and spills out of the top. Over time the lava hardens into rock. This builds up the volcano in layers. Lava flowing from these volcanoes can be spectacular looking.

Composite volcanoes are sometimes known as stratovolcanoes. They are taller and cone-shaped. They erupt violently with ash, gases, and **debris** instead of bubbling lava.

Plates and a Ring

The earth's crust is made of seven large **plates** that are broken into smaller plates. These plates fit together like puzzle pieces. The plates move and shift a lot in the areas where they meet. Many earthquakes happen where the plates hit

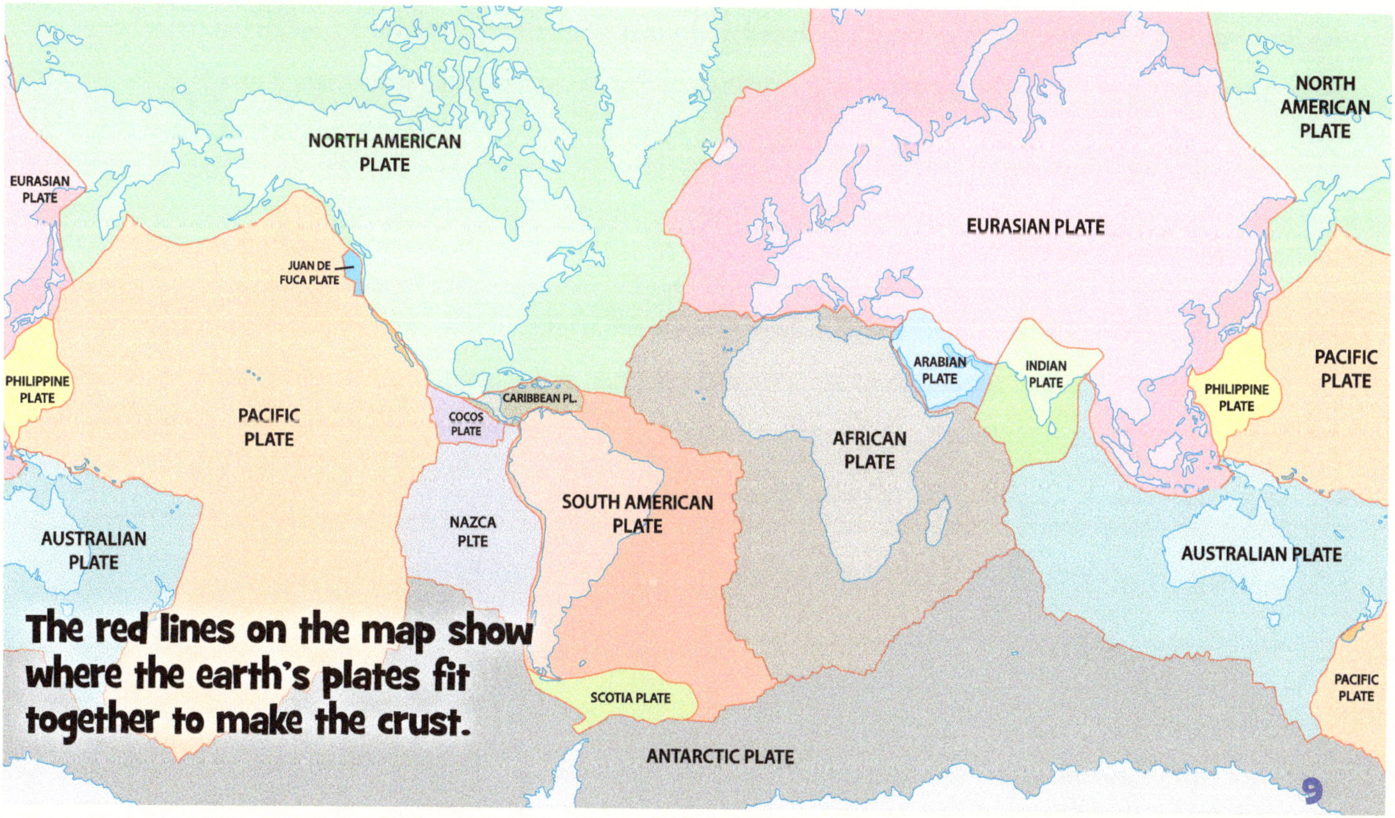

The red lines on the map show where the earth's plates fit together to make the crust.

together. Many mountains and volcanoes form there, too. During this activity, one plate shifts down while the other pushes up. These areas where large blocks of land push against each other are called **faults**.

The Ring of Fire

More than 75 percent of the earth's active volcanoes are found in one explosive area of the world. The Ring of Fire stretches around the Pacific Ocean. It's an area where the earth's crust moves and shifts more than in any other area of the world.

Mount Tambora

The Ring of Fire contains large strings of islands. Indonesia is made up of thousands of small islands. On one of these islands is a composite volcano called Mount Tambora.

Mount Tambora is known for a huge eruption in April of 1815. With very little warning, ash and rock were blown miles into the air. The eruption reached as far as 800 miles (1,287 kilometers) away and lasted for days.

A view from the rim of Mount Tambora's crater. It was created after the 1815 eruption.

Blowing Its Top

During the 1815 eruption, a 4,000-foot (1,219-meter) chunk of rock blew off Mount Tambora. This formed a huge crater and reduced the size of the mountain.

The blast killed more than ten thousand people. Another eighty-two thousand died later from disease and hunger. The ash even blocked the sun. Many parts of the world were cold for months and could not grow crops. The following year, 1816, became known as "the year without a summer."

Island Makers

Much of the 25,000-mile (40,000-km) Ring of Fire is under the Pacific Ocean. That means most of the earth's volcanoes in this area are on the ocean floor. Many composite volcanoes start on the ocean floor. New eruptions make the volcanoes larger and larger until they are above water. The Ring of Fire contains more volcanic islands than anywhere in the world.

These volcanoes are located in East Java, Indonesia. This country has some of the most active volcanoes in the Pacific Ring of Fire.

Life on a Volcano

About 170 people live in Aogashima, Japan, a 1-mile-square (3-km-square) volcanic island. The crater in the center gives off a smell of volcanic gases. And most of the remote island gets no internet or cell phone service.

The Hawaiian Islands

Not all volcanic islands form at the edges of the earth's plates. The Hawaiian Islands started forming over five million years ago, right in the middle of a plate. The chain of eight islands formed over a **hot spot** on the ocean floor. A hot spot is an area deep under the crust. Heat from the hot spot melts rock. It creates a crack in the crust that eventually becomes a volcano.

Remember that the earth's plates are always moving. As the plate moves, the hot spot stays in the same place. So, an old volcano shifts off the hot spot. A new area of the crust moves over the hot spot. A new volcano begins forming there. The Hawaiian Islands formed one by one as they each moved over the same hot spot under the crust.

Hawaii was formed by underwater volcanic activity. The brown areas on the Big Island mark the largest volcanoes (Mauna Loa and Mauna Kea).

Mauna Loa is 13,100 feet (4 km) above sea level. Its last eruption was in 1984.

Mauna Loa

The largest active volcano on the planet is part of the Hawaiian Islands. Mauna Loa means "Long Mountain" in Hawaiian. It covers half of the island of Hawaii. It's also very active. Since its first recorded eruption in 1868, it has erupted thirty-three times. The last time was in 1984.

Scientists place volcanoes into three groups based on how often they erupt. Active volcanoes erupt regularly, like Mauna Loa. Dormant volcanoes have not erupted for more than two hundred years. Extinct volcanoes no longer erupt. The Hawaiian Islands have all three kinds of volcanoes.

Nature Returns

Volcanic eruptions can cause terrible damage to a landscape. Trees and plants can be destroyed by ash, debris, and lava within minutes. Landslides of rock can change a landscape forever. Layers of ash can cover everything. Animals cannot live in the lakes or streams.

These two images show Mount Saint Helens before and after its 1980 eruption.

But volcanic eruptions also have benefits for the planet. Ash from a volcano is rich in nutrients. It helps plants regrow well. Over time, the landscape will recover. First, small plants grow back. Then larger plants and trees grow back.

These young plants are beginning to grow back in the middle of a field of hardened lava.

Avalanche!

When Mount Saint Helens erupted in 1980, part of the mountain slid away. It caused the biggest avalanche in recorded history. Debris sped down the mountain at 300 miles (482 km) per hour.

Animals Return

Once plants return to an **ecosystem**, animals will not be far behind. They rely on the plants for food and shelter. Birds and insects return to the area. Then mammals return as well. It can take many years, but the entire ecosystem will return.

Volcanoes continue to change the landscape over time. Mountains get built up with hardened lava. They get blown apart in eruptions. Volcanoes show the power of nature.

Activity: Model a Hot Spot

Use paper models to demonstrate how a hot spot can form a volcano.

You will need:

- orange sticky note
- tracing paper
- paper
- scissors

1. Place the sticky note on a table. The sticky note is the hot spot.
2. Place the tracing paper over the sticky note. The paper is the earth's crust.
3. Draw a circle over the section of tracing paper that is over the sticky note. Draw a volcano in the circle.
4. Very slowly slide the "crust" over the "hot spot." Stop after a few seconds. Draw another circle and volcano.
5. Continue until the entire tracing paper has moved over the hot spot. Color in your chain of volcanic islands!

A plate shifts over a hot spot. New volcanoes can form as the plate moves.

Learn More

Books

Chad, Jon. ***Volcanoes: Fire and Life***. New York, NY: Roaring Brook Press, 2016.

Galat, Joan. ***Erupt! 100 Fun Facts About Volcanoes***. Washington, DC: National Geographic, 2017.

Ganeri, Anita. ***Eruption! The Story of Volcanoes***. London, UK: Dorling Kindersley, 2015.

Websites

Ready.gov

www.ready.gov/volcanoes

Read about how people who live near active volcanoes can prepare for and stay safe during an eruption.

Volcano: National Geographic Kids

kids.nationalgeographic.com/explore/science/volcano/#volcano-explode.jpg

Learn more about volcanoes, how they form, and the damage they can do.

Index

Published in 2020 by Enslow Publishing, LLC.
101 W. 23rd Street, Suite 240, New York, NY 10011

Library of Congress Cataloging-in-Publication Data
Names: Furgang, Kathy, author.
Title: Volcanoes / Kathy Furgang.
Description: New York : Enslow Publishing, 2020. | Series: Investigate earth science | Audience: K to grade 4. | Includes bibliographical references and index.
Identifiers: LCCN 2018052067| ISBN 9781978507401 (library bound) | ISBN 9781978508743 (pbk.) | ISBN 9781978508750 (6 pack)
Subjects: LCSH: Volcanoes—Juvenile literature. | Plate tectonics—Juvenile literature.
Classification: LCC QE521.3 .F8745 2020 | DDC 551.21—dc23
LC record available at https://lccn.loc.gov/2018052067

Printed in the United States of America

Photos Credits: Cover, p. 1 LukaKikina/Shutterstock.com; pp. 3, 6 Sara Hahn/Shutterstock.com; pp. 3, 7 Designua/Shutterstock.com; pp. 3, 9 Rainer Lesniewski/Shutterstock.com; pp. 3, 15 Bardocz Peter/Shutterstock.com; pp. 3, 18–19 Everett Collection Inc/Alamy Stock Photo; p. 5 Sebastián Crespo Photography/Moment/Getty Images; p. 11 Mangiwau/Moment Open/Getty Images; p. 13 Benjawan Sittidech/Moment/Getty Images; p. 16 Joe Carini/Perspectives/Getty Images; p. 20 morrowdeana/iStock/Getty Images Plus/Getty Images; p. 23 QAI Publishing/Universal Images Group/Getty Images; cover graphics blackpencil/Shutterstock.com.